You make the world Special just Because You're in it.

Pax,
Ron

# You Are You, You Are Special: A Story of Belonging

Ronald B. Cox
Illustrated by Barbara J. Saxe

You Are You, You Are Special:

A Story of Belonging



PastorRonDevotional@gmail.com



Printed in the United States of America

THIS BOOK BELONGS TO

***Not belonging is a terrible feeling. It feels awkward, and it hurts as if you were wearing someone else's shoes.***

***Phoebe Stone***

***Feeling invisible is the worst feeling in the world.***

***RBC***

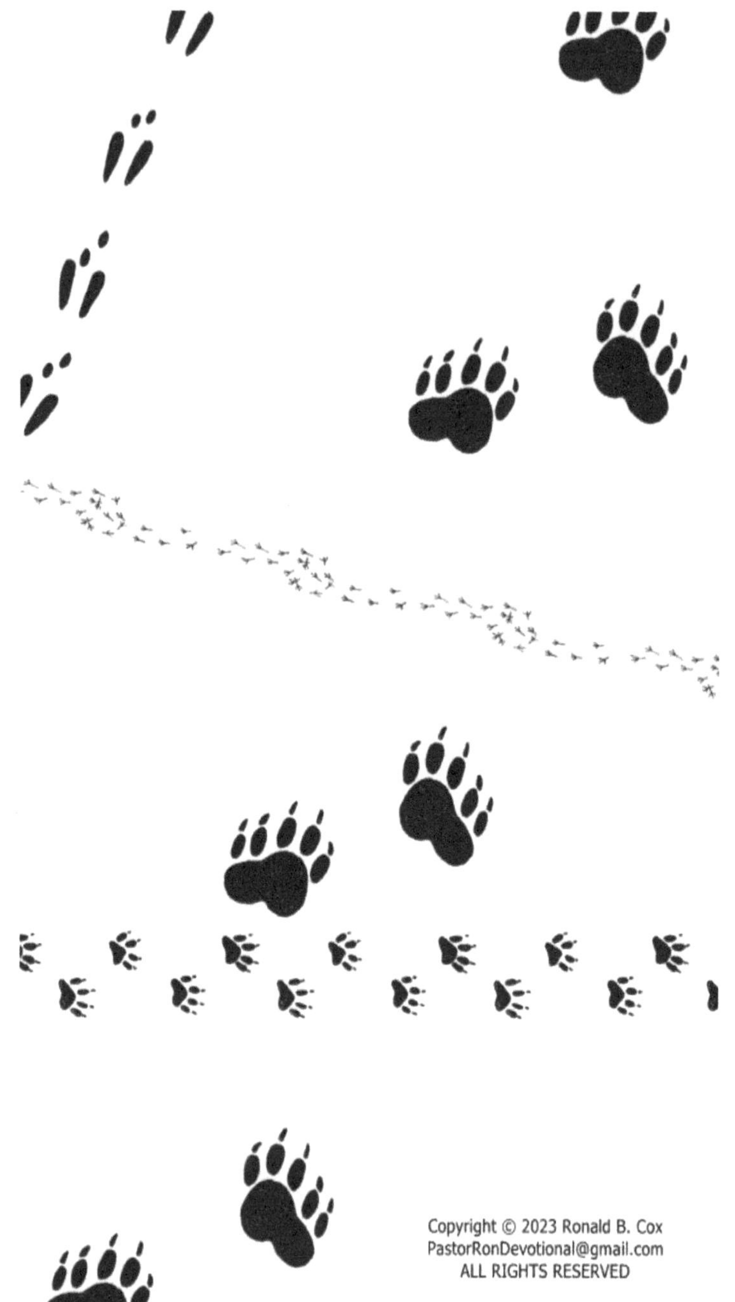

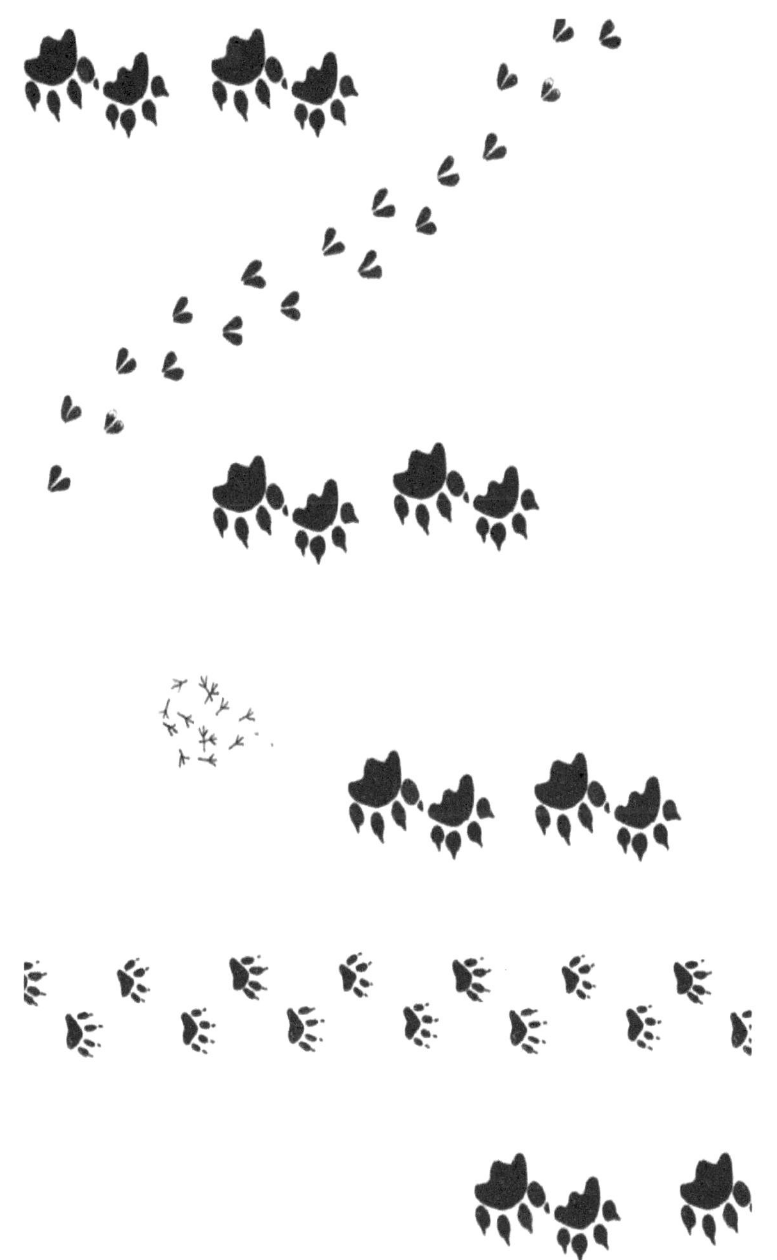

# TABLE OF CONTENTS

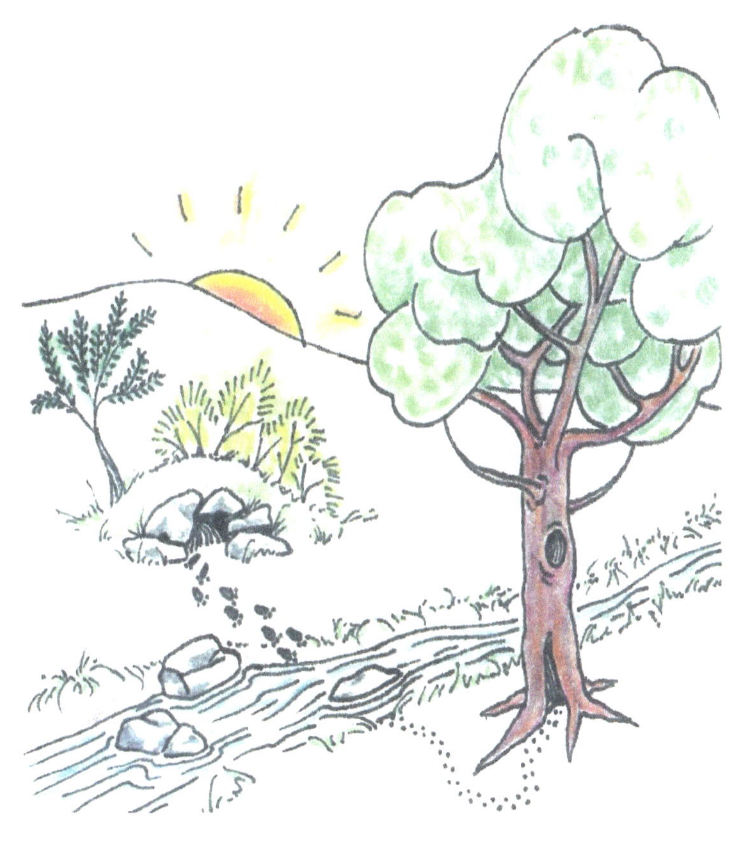

# CHAPTER 1

In the beginning, before time as we know it, there was

a land called Bustani where all animals lived together happily. Every animal you can imagine lived peacefully with all other animals. No animals went hungry, and there was water, shade, and places for every creature to live. If animals chased each other, it was to play, not to kill. Animals of all shapes and sizes, and kinds lived and played together as one happy family. You could say, "This was perfect."

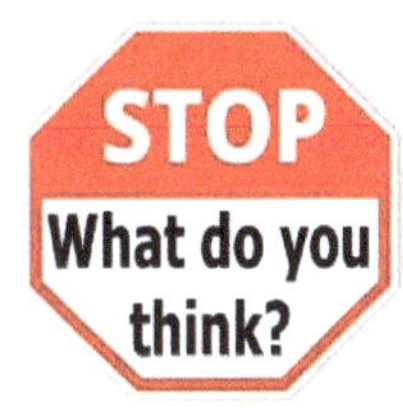


***What would it be like to live in a world where everyone lives peacefully with each other?***

## CHAPTER 2

But, sadly, it wasn't. You see, there were these little twins, Diya and Daya. They wanted badly to have friends to play with, but were always shut out. They would try day after day with no success because they and their family looked different from everyone else. And because of this, all the other little ones made fun of them.

Sometimes other little ones would bully Diya and Daya by ignoring them. They would be called names, and when it came time to play a game, they were never asked to join. They actually felt invisible.

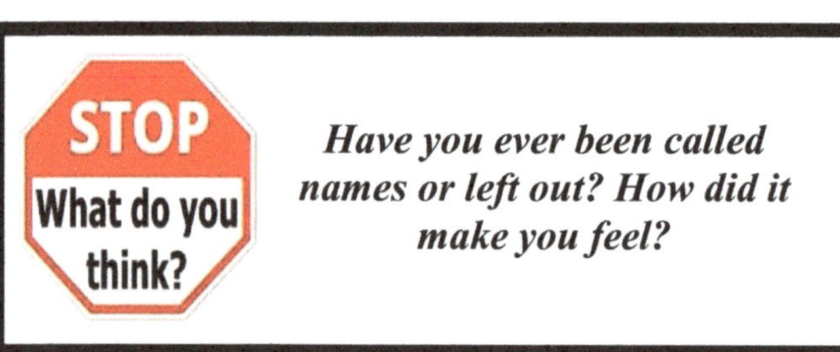

## CHAPTER 3

Diya and Daya asked their parents why no one would play with them.

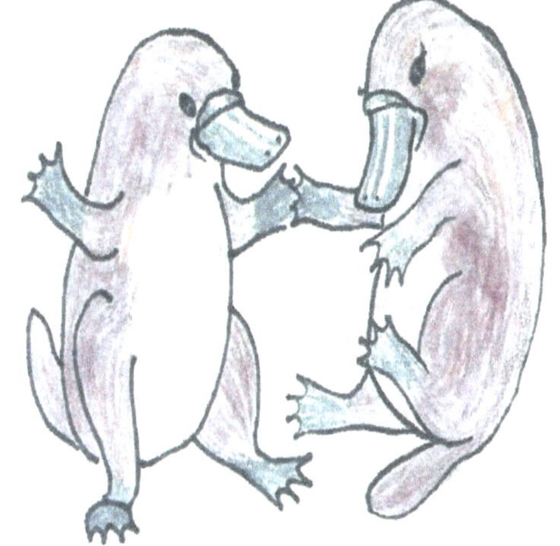

They asked them, “Why won’t anyone play with us? They make fun of the way we look.”

“Just Ignore them,” Khamisi replied, “You are beautiful in your own special way.”

Zuwena added, “Now go outside and enjoy the beautiful weather. We have work to do.”

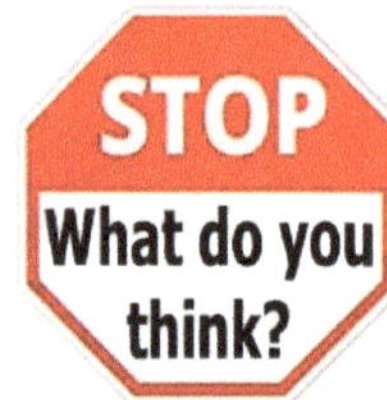


***Who are you able to go to with a problem; your parents, a teacher, a neighbor, or someone else?***

## CHAPTER 4

Listening to their parents, Diya and Daya looked at each other, shrugged, and went outside to play. As they skipped down by the river, they heard laughing and giggling in the distance. As they approached the bank

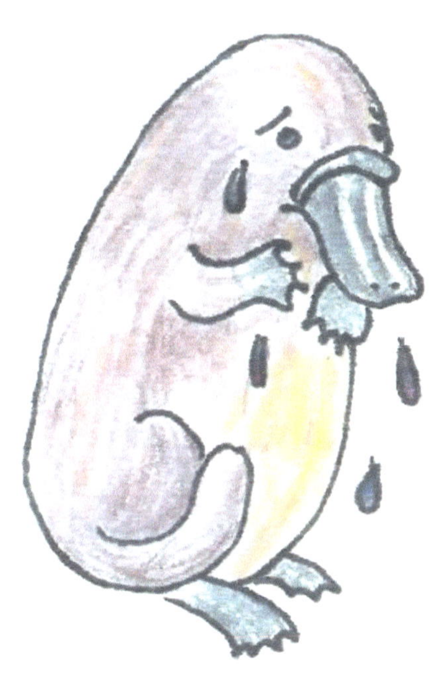

of the river, they saw a group of animals playing in the water. Diya said to Daya, "Let's ask if we can play with them.

Four or five are in my class at school."

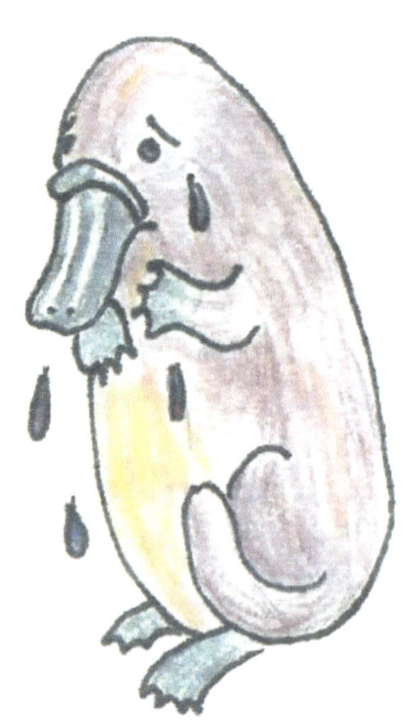

Daya was skeptical, but agreed. They walked up to the group, and Diya asked if they could join in. Hasira shouted, "We don't want to play with you. Just leave us alone." Little by little, the other animals began chanting, "LEAVE us alone! Leave US alone! Leave us ALONE!"

All the other animals turned their backs on Diya and Daya and laughed and called them names.

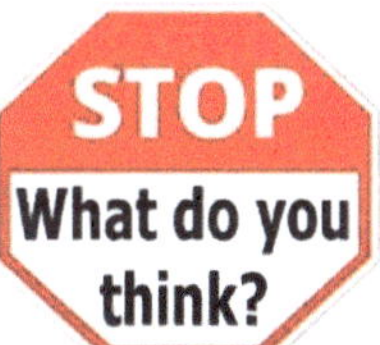


***Has anyone ever laughed at you because of the way you look or the way you talk?***

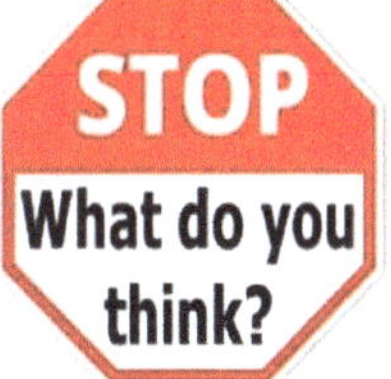


***Have you ever laughed at someone because of the way they looked or talked?***

## CHAPTER 5

Diya and Daya turned and ran away with tears flowing down their faces. They ran and ran until they came upon a large myrtle tree. As it happened, it was one of their favorite spots. There was a small opening a little above the base covered by leaves. It was special to them. They would often squeeze and huddle inside to read, make up stories, and dream about what it might be like to have friends. Right now, at this moment, it was a place for them to hide. It was their safe place. As they talked about what had just happened, they hugged each other and began to sob.

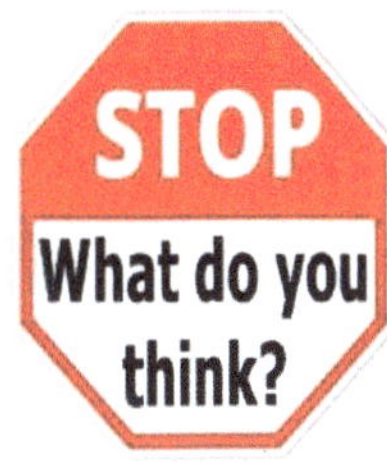


***Is there some place you go when you feel sad or alone?***

# CHAPTER 6

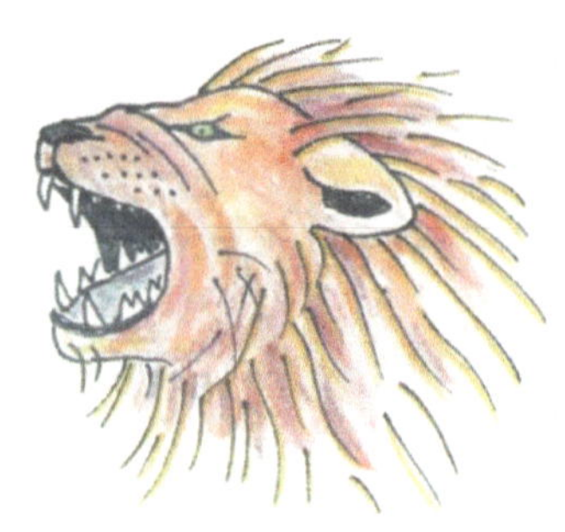

Akina and Jabali, the leaders of Bustani, were walking together, making preparations for a celebration that was to begin on the evening of the next full moon. Not thinking so much about where they were going, they just happened to be passing the

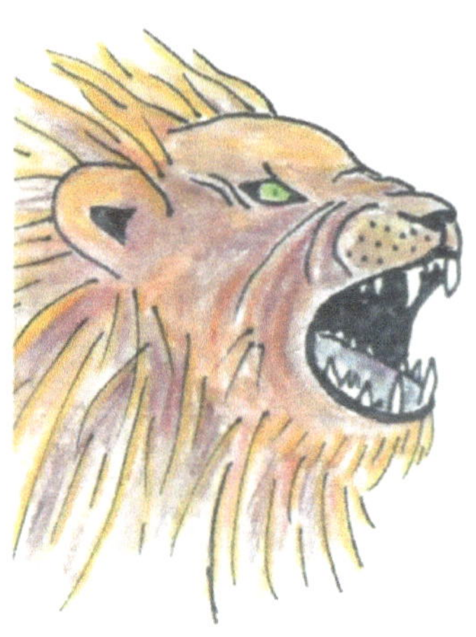

exact Myrtle tree where Diya and Daya were hiding.

Akina and Jabali, full-grown lions, were the chosen leaders of the land. Not because they were big and strong, but because they made it their business to make sure everyone was happy and stayed healthy.

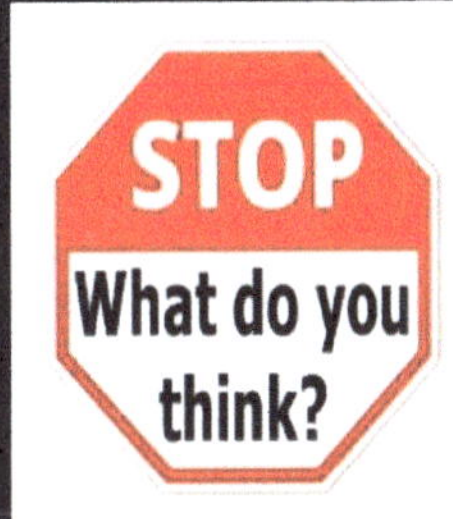


*Who are the grownups you can trust?*

## CHAPTER 7

Passing by the myrtle tree, Akina stopped... listened closely ... and said, "Do you hear that, Jabali?" Listening carefully, Jabali responded, "I think I do, Akina. I hear crying. I wonder what's wrong. No one should be sad and crying on such a

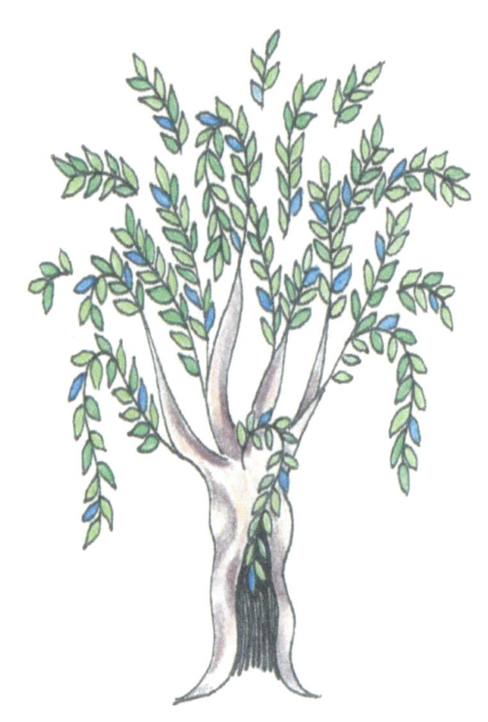

beautiful day as today." Together they looked up and down the tree and yet saw no one. As they walked around the tree, Akina said, "I think the crying is coming from inside." As they listened more intently, they followed the sound of crying to a branch covered with leaves. Akina pushed the leaves aside and discovered Diya and Daya huddled together. Looking at Diya, Akina looked in and asked, "My child, why are you so sad? Why are you crying?"

"This is such a beautiful day," said Jabali. "This is not a day for tears. Why are you and Daya not out playing with all the other little ones? Please come out so we can talk." Being obedient little animals, they came out of their hiding place and stood before Jabali and Akina.

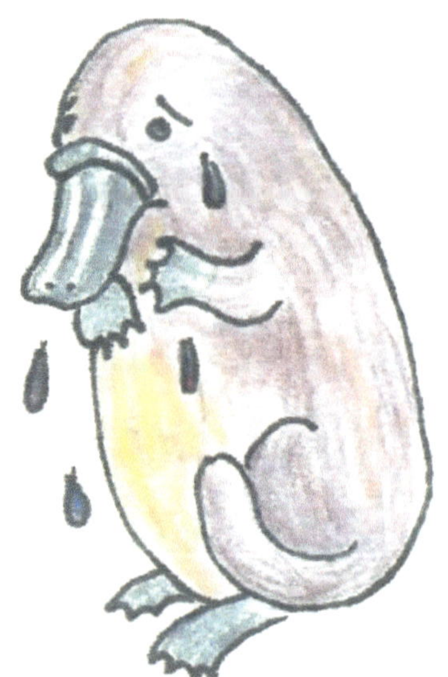

"What is the matter, my little ones?" asked Jabali.

Taking a deep, long breath, Diya replied, "No one will play with us. All the other little animals call us names and make fun of us."

"Why would you say that my child?" answered Jabali.

"Because," Daya blurted out, "we look different!"

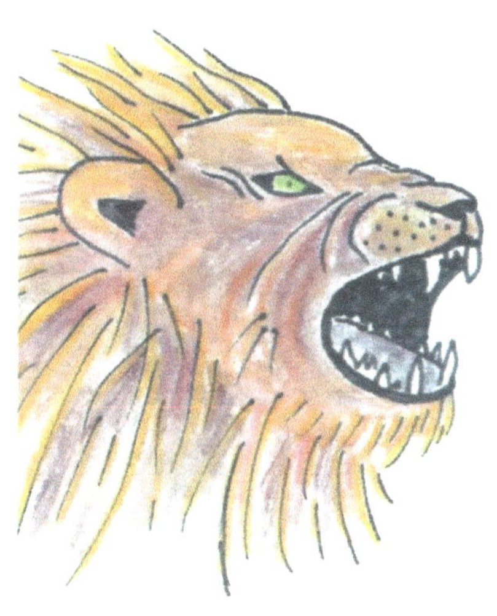

After hearing what Diya and Daya

had said, Akina and Jabali let out a deafening roar that was heard throughout the land. It was their way of calling all the animals to assemble in a beautiful meadow that was at the center of their world.

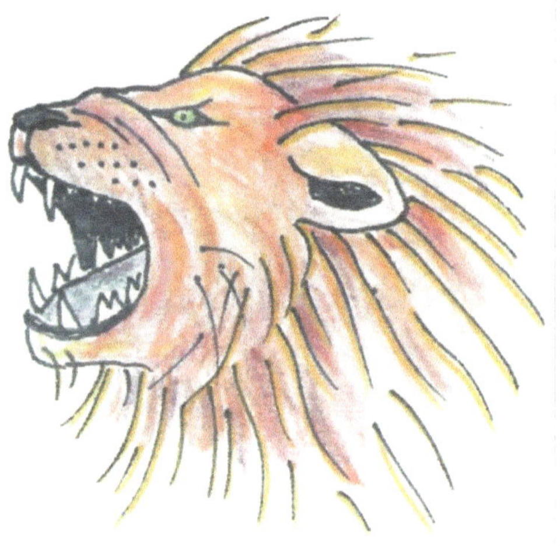

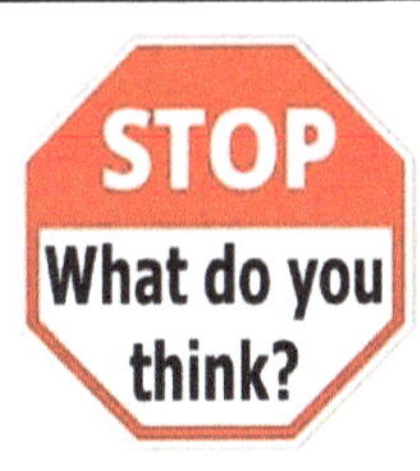


***When you talk to grownups, do you believe they understand how you feel?***

## CHAPTER 8

As the animals began to make their way to the meadow," Akina said, "Come with me, little ones. I will get to the bottom of this. No one should ever be made fun of because of how they look, act, speak or anything else."

So together, Akina, Jabali, Diya, and Daya walked to the center of the meadow where the most beautiful and majestic tree stood. It was called La Maisha, "The Tree of Life."

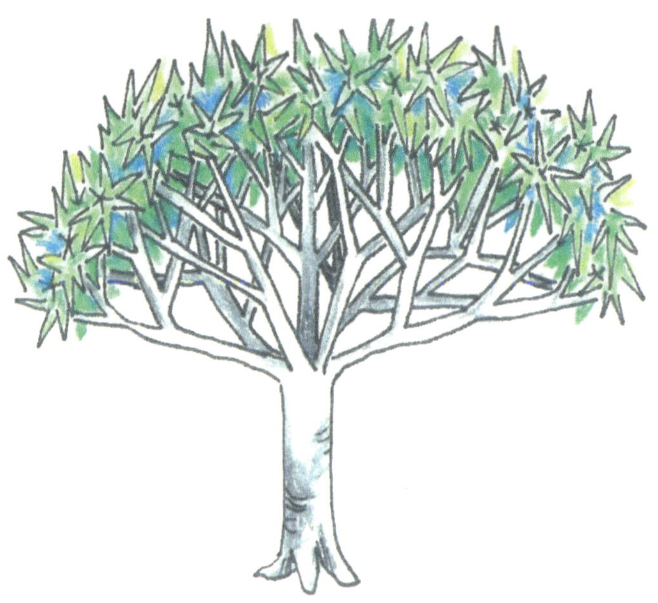

While the animals gathered, Jabali called the assembly to order, 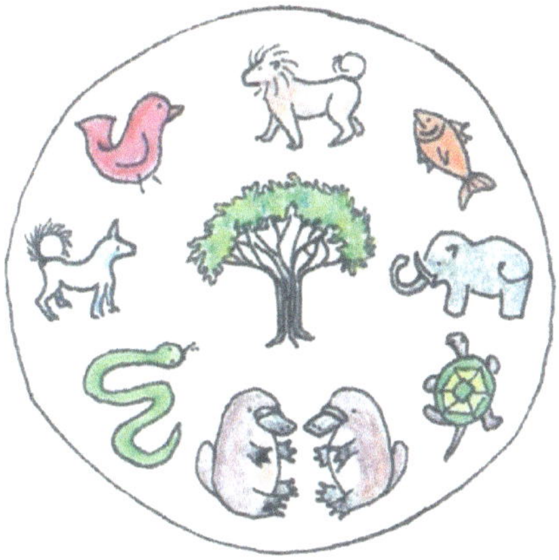
asking all to be silent and asking all the little ones to come and sit in the front. Akina and Jabali took turns telling everyone assembled what Diya and Daya had told them. They wanted an explanation of why this was happening. “Why is this so,” demanded Jabali. Looking at the little animals, Akina

asked, “Who will be the first to speak?”

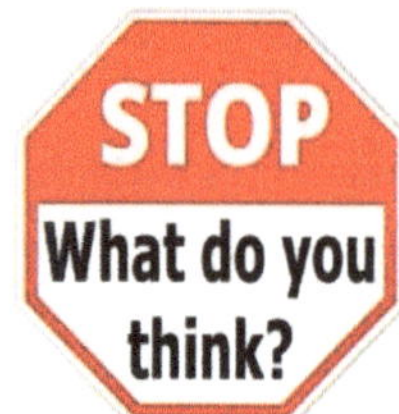


***What must it feel like to stand in front of a large group of people and have them talk about you?***

## CHAPTER 9

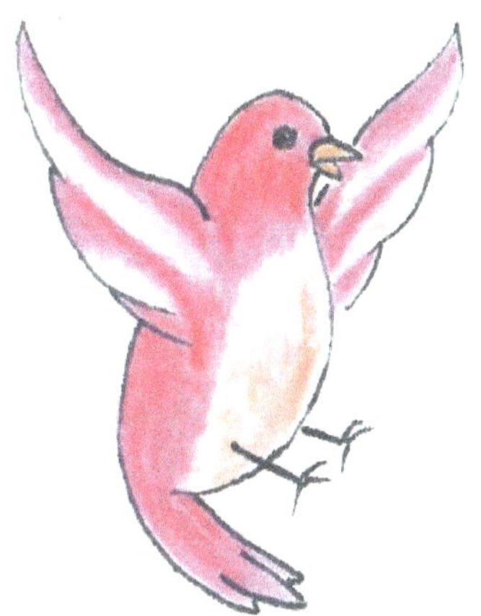

Manna was the first to speak up. “Even though they have

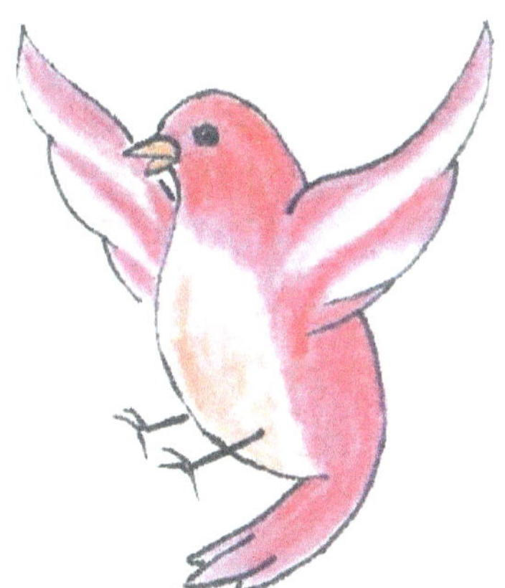

webbed feet, a bill, and lay eggs, they are not birds. They have no wings.

They look so funny. They need to find friends somewhere else."

Mkaidi was the next to weigh in. "Diya and Daya are clearly not reptiles. We are cold-blooded, they are not.

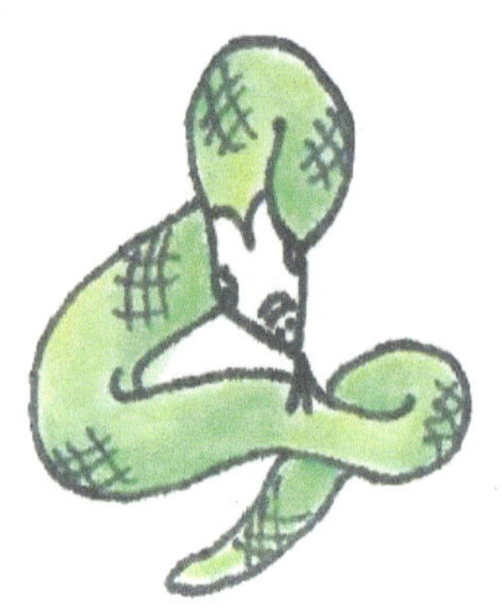

They are warm-blooded." Their bodies

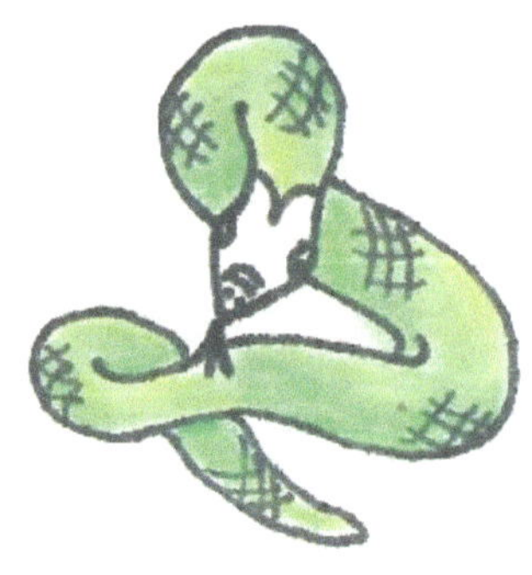

are covered with fur. Our bodies are covered with scales. There is no way Diya and Daya are reptiles. Besides, they just look so funny. They need to find friends somewhere else."

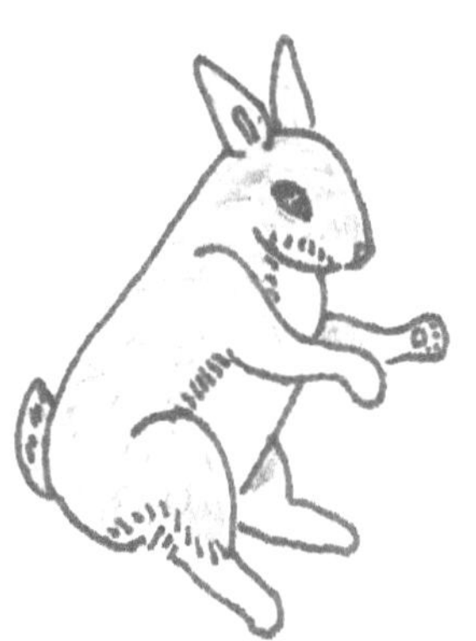

Si Rafiki chimed in. "We agree that they are warm-blooded and that that they have fur, and that they are fed warm milk from their mothers, but, it's something about the way they look. Look at them. They look so strange.

They need to find

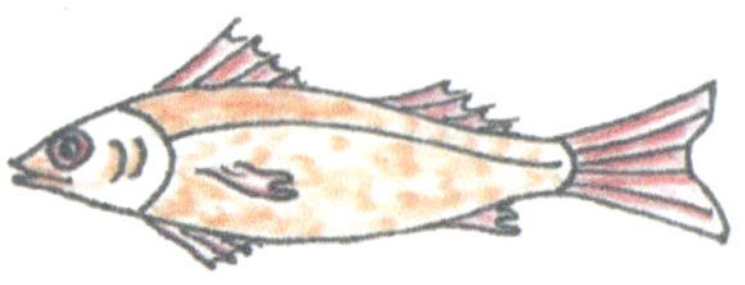

friends somewhere else. In fact, we have all agreed they are … actually fish." "What do mean?" interrupted

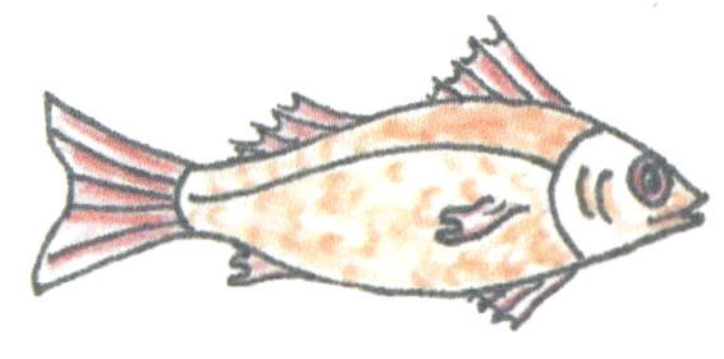

Mbaya. "Just because they swim and find their food in the water does not make them fish. They have no scales or gills.

They have lungs.  And look at that tail. Pointing at the beavers," Mbaya said, "That's where they belong!"

"Now, just you wait a minute," spoke up Bure. "I think not! A beaver's tail does not make a beaver. They do not eat the bark of trees and certainly do not live in a lodge in the middle of

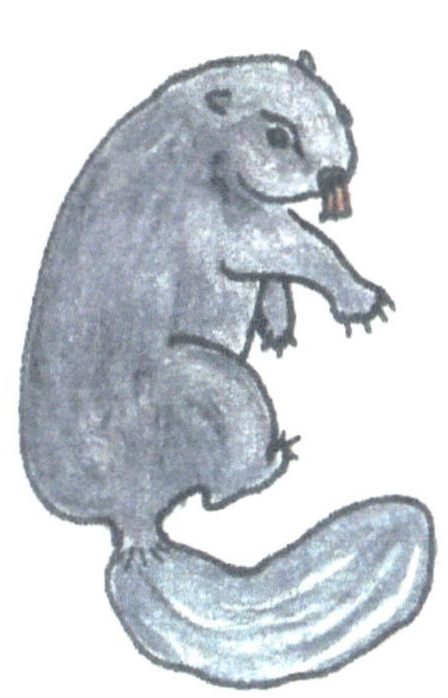

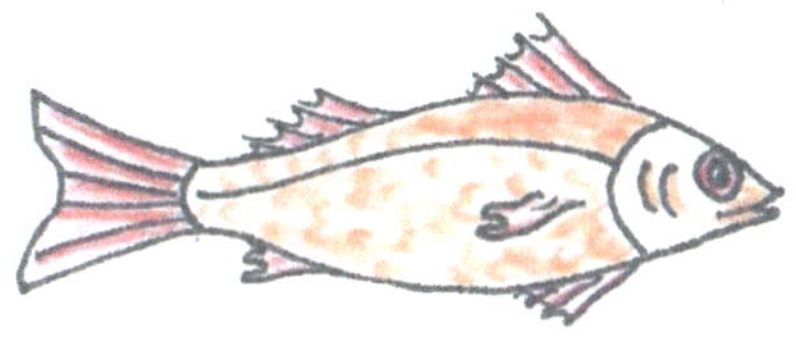

lakes, rivers,

and ponds. To suggest that they are beavers is just wrong. They need to find friends somewhere else."

What had started as a peaceful meeting began to get out of control as arguments erupted among all the little ones and adult animals until finally Akina spoke... "Silence! I call for everyone to be silent!" Speaking to the adult animals, Akina said, "Jabali and I came across Diya and Daya in tears. They felt rejected by all the little ones and were not allowed to play with their young. AND... they were even called names and made fun of just because of the way they look." Jabali added, "My heart breaks for them. Why should that be? What makes all of you better than these two? How would you feel if your little ones had no friends? How dare you!"

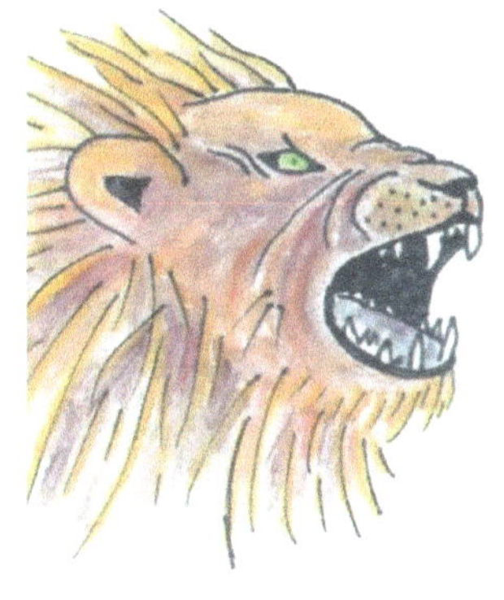

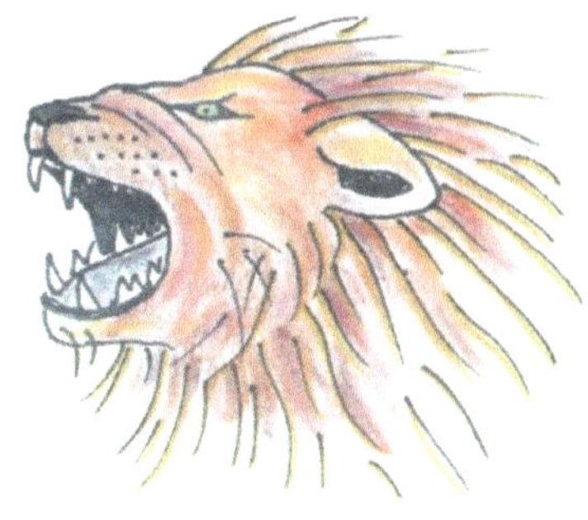

From the back of the assembled animals, Kiburi was heard to say, "But they don't look like any of us. They look so strange. They are different."

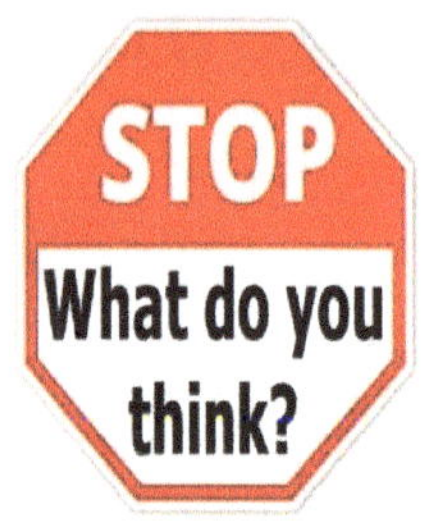


***When you meet someone, what do you look at first: how they dress, how they talk, the color of their hair or skin, or something else?***

## CHAPTER 10

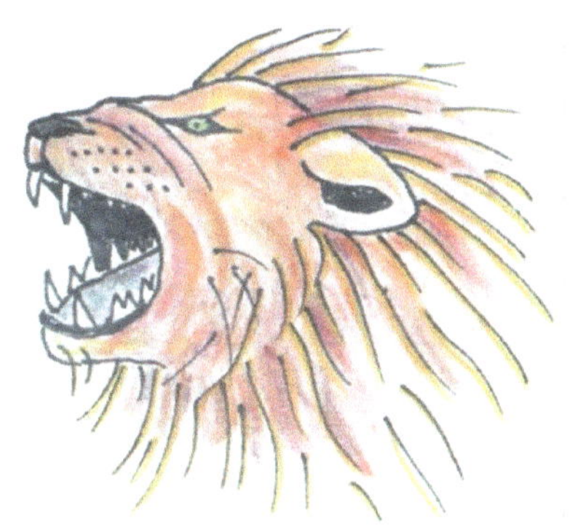

Enraged and bursting with anger, Akina and Jabali roared with such intensity that the sound seemed to shake creation at its very core.

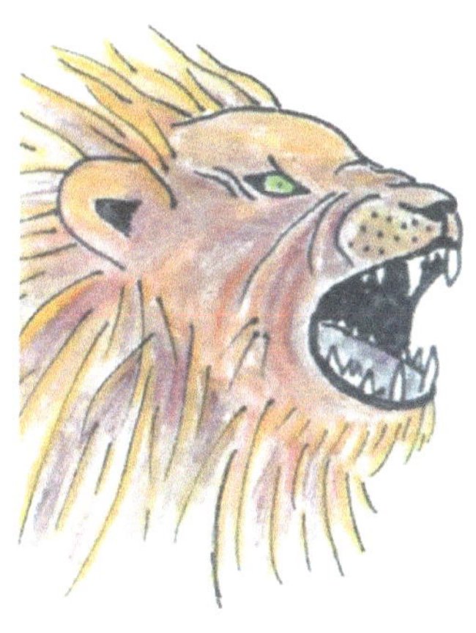

Together they lifted their heads and commanded, "SILENCE!" In that moment, not a sound was to be heard except the whistling of the wind. Jabali said, “How dare you judge someone else by what they look like, or how they speak, or how they think or act. I always thought that it was our differences that make

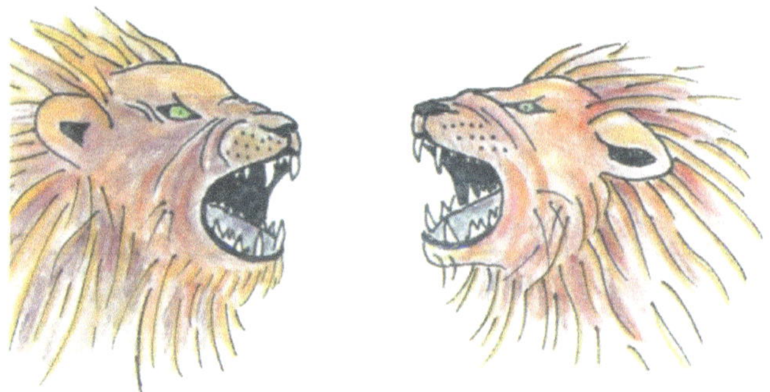

us special.” Akina added, “We need to celebrate our differences. Jabali and I would say that Diya and

Daya represent all of us because there is a little bit of everyone in them. They are not different from us... they are us! In many ways, they show us what a family should be like...different, but the same." Akina and Jabali looked at each other and then at all the animals gathered and said, "Remember, everyone belongs."

After they spoke, there was a deep silence among all the animal families. They began to feel ashamed of the way their little ones had acted toward the twins as well as themselves for not seeing the problem. And then, as if on cue, all the little ones ran to Diya and Daya and said, "We are so, so sorry. Let us try to be friends."

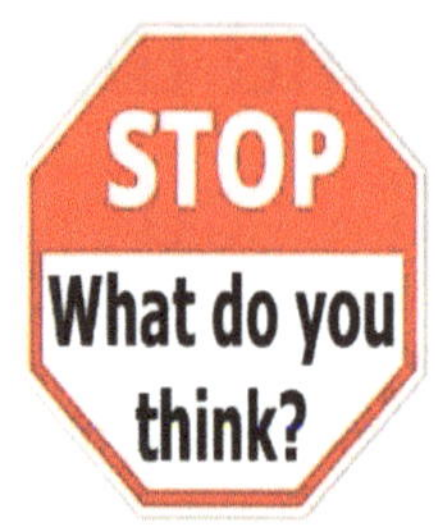


***What must it feel like to have someone stand up for you? Do you agree with what Akina and Jabali said to the animals?***

## CHAPTER 11

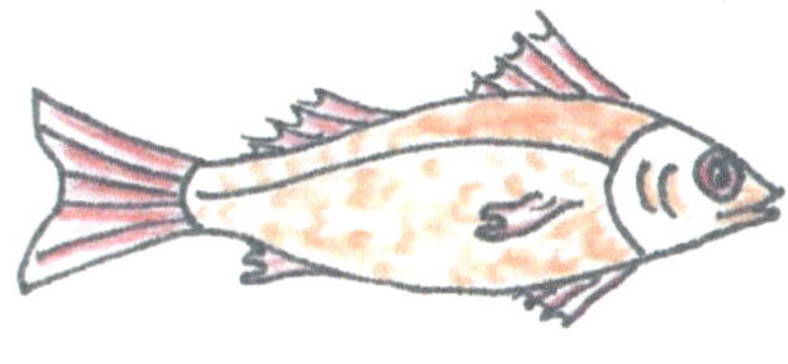

As time went on, little by little, Diya and Daya began to feel more accepted because they were asked to join in the games and all the other activities.

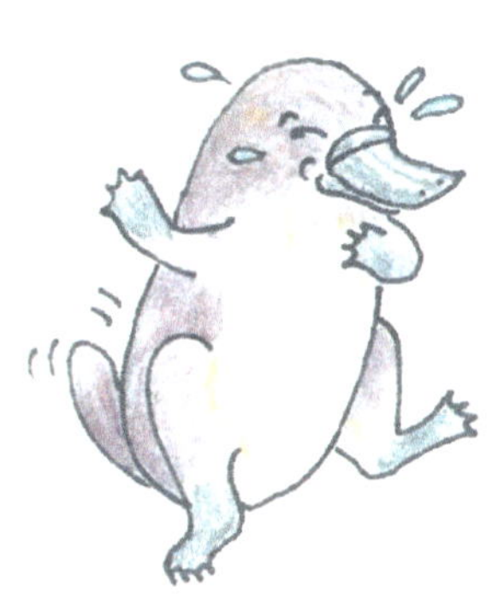

Their tears of sadness had turned into tears of happiness. They no

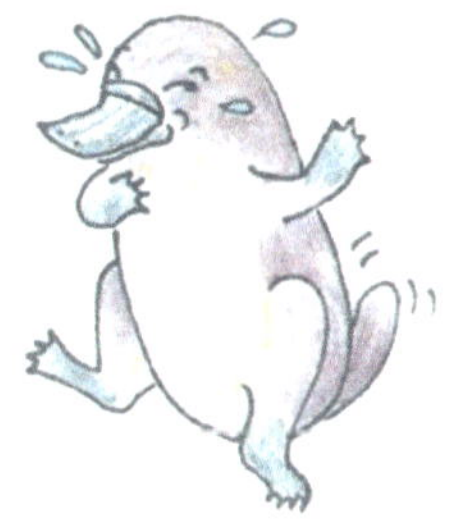

longer felt invisible and left out. It was amazing how the other animals, young and old, began to see with new eyes. They realized just because someone looked different. It doesn't make any difference at all. For the first time in their lives, the twins felt welcomed and happy. Not because of how they looked, but because of who they were.

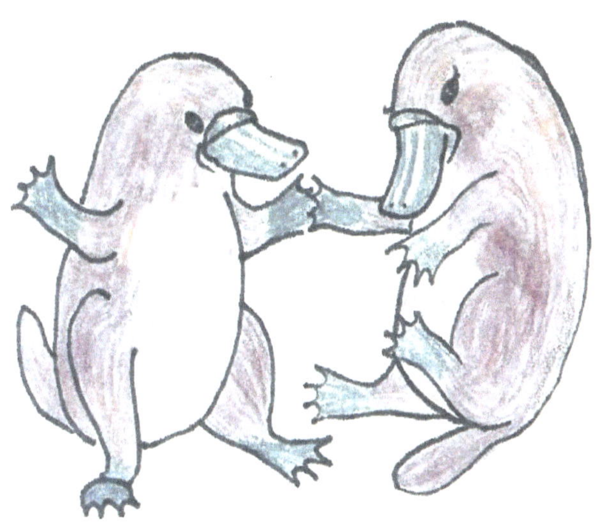

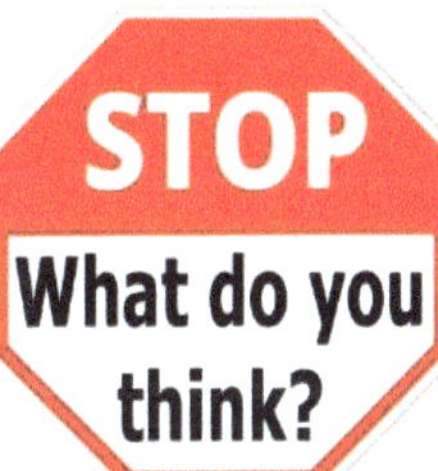


***Why do you think this story has a happy ending? What is more important, what someone looks like or what they are in inside? Is there someone in school or where you live that might feel left out?***

## SING-A-LONG

# "You Are You, You Are Special"

You are you,
    You are special,
There is no one in the world
    that's just like you.

Don't be afraid
    You make the world a better place;
Because you're special.
    You are you.

You are you,
    You are exceptional,
There will never be another one like you.
    Be confident in all you say and all you do,
Because you're special.
    You are you.

**SCAN TO ACCESS THE SONG**

# WHAT IS THE MORAL OF THE STORY?

*The moral of a story is the lesson that the story teaches about how to behave in the world and be a better person.*

This story has a moral.

Instead of me telling you what I think the moral is, I would like you to dig inside of yourself and see if you can discover what you believe is the moral of the story.

Here is a suggestion: Imagine you are Diya or Daya. What did you learn on your journey that finally led you to have some friends and feel like you belonged? You could also imagine you are the bird, Manna, or any of the other characters. It just might be possible that you will discover that each character may have a different moral.

Don't be afraid to say out loud what you are thinking. There is no right or wrong answer. The moral of the story is what you learned from traveling with Diya and Daya on their journey to belong.

# WHO'S WHO

NAMES AND MEANINGS
(In order of appearance in story)

Diya . . . . . . . . . . . . . . . . . . . . Light
Daya . . . . . . . . . . . . . . . . . .Compassion
Khamisi . . . . . . . . . . . . . .Good
Zuwena . . . . . . . . . Born on Thursday
Hasira . . . . . . . . . . . . . . . . .. Unkind
Akina . . . . . . . . . . . . . . . . . . Unity
Jabali . . . . . . . . . . . . . . Strong as a Rock
Manna . . . . . . . . . . . . . Mean
Mkaidi . . . . . . . . . . . . . Bully
Si Rafiki . . . . . . . . . . Unfriendly
Mbaya . . . . . . . . . . . . . Nasty
Bure . . . . . . . . . . . . . . . Vain
Kiburi . . . . . . . . . . . . . . . . Arrogant

# PLACES AND THINGS

NAMES AND MEANINGS
(In order of appearance in story)

Bustani . . . . . . . . . . . . . . . . . . . . . . . . Garden
Myrtle Tree. . . . . .Symbolizes love and good luck
La Maisha . . . . . . . . . . . . . . . . Tree of Life

# DO YOU LIKE TO COLOR?

The games and coloring pages can be downloaded for copying by using the QR Code and following the link.

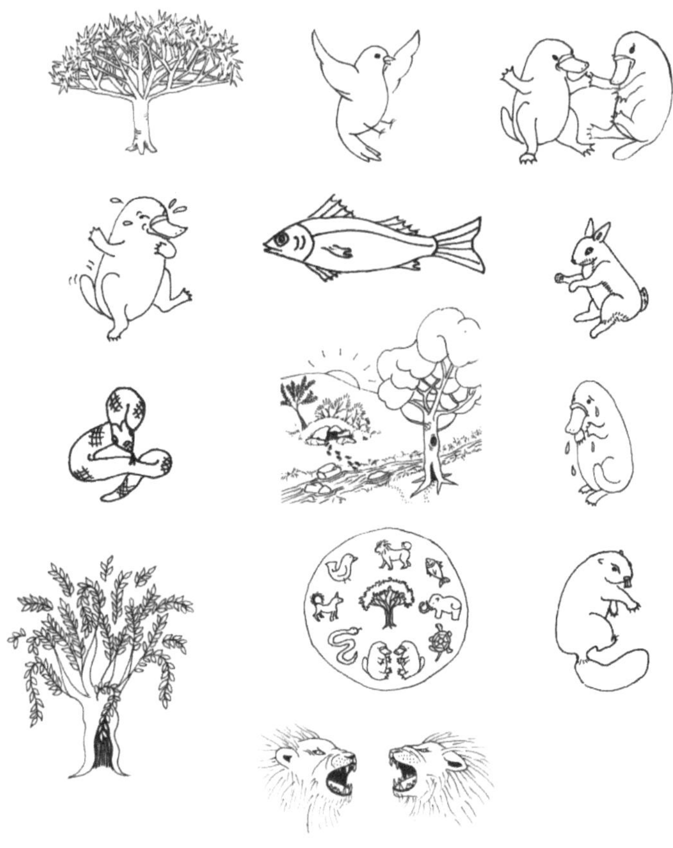

# DO YOU LIKE GAMES?

The games and coloring pages can be downloaded for copying by using the QR Code and following the link.

## CODE BUSTER

Use the Code Buster at the bottom of the page to decipher the sentence.

CODE BUSTER

| A | B | C | D | E | F | G | H | I | J | K | L | M |
|---|---|---|---|---|---|---|---|---|---|---|---|---|
| N | O | P | Q | R | S | T | U | V | W | X | Y | Z |

## WORD MAKER

The total number of word that can be made out of platypus = 125
Below are some of them. See how many you can discover.

2 LETTER WORDS (5 out of 11 possibilities)

3 LETTER WORDS (12 out of 40 possibilities)

4 LETTER WORDS (10 out of 42 possibilities)

5 LETTER WORDS (2 out of 28 possibilities)

6 LETTER WORDS (1 out of 4 possibilities)

## SEEK AND FIND

A K F Z P Y K C S A N M J H G F F D
F J I C O O J G F A N L K J H G C X
H H S Y O U A R E S P E C I A L O T
Y G H X I A H H D T G H D G H J K G
R B S C U R G J G O V M F W E E K V
K E D V T E A R S R I Y T H J K O C
Z A F B Y Y F K H Y T R A B B I T P
M V G N T O D L J O Y T D E R F G Y
O E H M R U S R I F R L J P G H R T
T R J S N A K E O B B E B P H O P J
F N D I Y A A T Y E R T T A K I N A
G F W D E Y M Y T L T R C R T C Y B
J D E F W A N U G O R E T E H G F A
E J R G Q D B I H N A E S N D F G L
G L A M A I S H A G V Z D T T L J I
I K R B U S T A N I F L K S J U I P
D O T T L F V O N N A N I M A L S B
N P Y Y K G C R M G T G B V F R E D
H R U U A S D F G A M J H G F D G Y

AKINA
A STORY OF BELONGING
ANIMALS
BEAVER
BUSTANI
DAYA
DIYA
FISH
JABALI
JOY
LA MAISHA
MYRTLE TREE
PARENTS
RABBIT
SNAKE
TEARS
YOU ARE SPECIAL
YOU ARE YOU

## CROSSWORD PUZZLE

**Across**

2. Flying animal
5. Animal with special tail
8. Name of leader
9. Name of 2nd leader
11. Hiding place
12. Tree of Life
13. What kind of animals were the leaders

**Down**

1. Reptile in story
2. Land called
3. Mammal in story
4. Name of 2nd twin
6. Name of twin
7. What kind of animal are the twins
10. Where is Tree of Life

# PARENT'S PAGE

"You Are You, You Are Special: A Story of Belonging" is an allegorical tale about a set of twins who have been ignored, made fun of, and ostracized because of the way they looked, which resulted in feeling unwanted and invisible.

Growing up has always been difficult. I would suggest that it is even harder today. As a former teacher and a retired minister, I am a firm believer that in order to 'Become' a child needs to 'Belong.'

I wrote this story as a way for families to begin having a conversation around the topic of belonging. It could be helpful for a child who feels on the 'outs.' And it also has the potential to sensitize your child as to how other children may be experiencing their life in school or at play.

I would propose the best way to use this little book is for you to read the story aloud with your child. Included at the end of each chapter is a question or two. Before proceeding to the next chapter, take a moment to stop, pause, reflect, and discuss.

At present, when attention is constantly being drawn to our differences, I am hoping this little story will help draw us to recognize our sameness.

It is my hope that this little allegorical story might help make a difference in the life of your most precious gift, your child.

*"Books are the mirrors of the soul." Virginia Woolf*

# MOTTO TO LIVE BY

A motto is a slogan or favorite saying, like "*Everyone Belongs.*" A motto is something you might see on a t-shirt or bumper sticker. It is a short sentence or phrase that has meaning for that person.

Here are some famous mottos.

> *"Don't Worry, Be Happy"*
>
> *"Don't sweat the small stuff."*
>
> *"Be Yourself"*
>
> *"Honesty is the best policy."*
>
> *"Be kind."*
>
> *"Make every day count."*

MY CHALLENGE FOR YOU:

1) Can you make up a sentence or phrase that could become your motto?
2) Is that motto something you could put on a t-shirt to let the whole world see?
3) What does that motto say about you?

# MUSIC LEAD SHEET

## YOU ARE YOU, YOU ARE SPECIAL

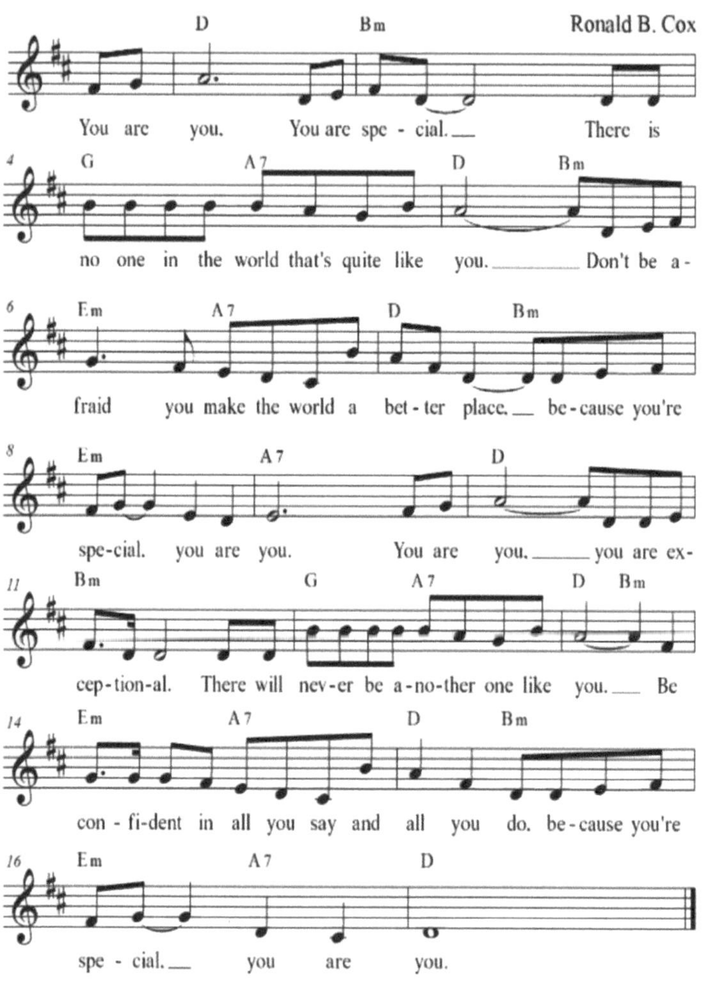



PastorRonDevotional@gmail.com

# ACKNOWLEDGEMENTS

I would like to express my sincere appreciation to the following people who have been so gracious in helping this tiny story come into its final form.

Thank you.
Ron

Faye Tiger Conquest, Guidance Counselor
Luke E. DiMaria, Business Owner
Mary Hogan, Director of the
Coral J. Belden Library
Maria Librio-Judge, Business Owner
Sharon June, Reading Specialist
David Robson, Playwright
Barbara J. Saxe, Illustrator
William Saxe, English Teacher
and most importantly, my wife, Jeanie.

RONALD B. COX, Writer of story, music, and lyrics

Ron is the father of three daughters and seven grandchildren. He, and his wife, Jean, have been married for 54 years and are presently retired in the Town of Rocky Hill, Connecticut. They both are graduates of Temple University College of Education in Philadelphia, Pennsylvania. Following many years in teaching, Ron and Jean attended seminary and were both ordained. As a teacher, cleric, composer, and community activist, Ron has spent his adult career assisting people of all ages, but especially children, to find a sense of purpose and value.

BARBARA J. SAXE, Illustrator

Barbara is an inveterate doodler who studied watercolor with William Carbone and has exhibited locally. She lives in the Catskill mountains with her husband and takes inspiration from everything around her.